LTL

1/04

North American Indians Today

North American Indians Today

- Apache
- Cherokee
- Cheyenne
- Comanche
- Creek
- Crow
- Huron
- Iroquois
- Navajo
- Ojibwa
- Osage
- Potawatomi
- Pueblo
- Seminole
- Sioux

North American
Indians Today

Huron

by
Autumn Libal

Mason Crest Publishers
Philadelphia

We would like to thank the Wyandotte Nation of Oklahoma and Sainte-Marie among the Hurons for their help with this book. Special thanks to Jim Bland, Juanita McQuistion, Sherri Clemons, and all the other people who gave so generously of their time and knowledge.

Mason Crest Publishers Inc.
370 Reed Road
Broomall, Pennsylvania 19008
(866) MCP-BOOK (toll free)

First printing
1 2 3 4 5 6 7 8 9 10
Library of Congress Cataloging-in-Publication Data on file at the Library of Congress.
ISBN: 1-59084-670-2
1-59084-663-X (series)

Design by Lori Holland.
Composition by Bytheway Publishing Services, Binghamton, New York.
Cover design by Benjamin Stewart.
Printed and bound in the Hashemite Kingdom of Jordan.

Photography by Benjamin Stewart except as noted in captions; pp. 72, 87 PhotoDisc.

Contents

Why is it so important that Indians be brought into the "mainstream" of American life?
I would not know how to interpret this phrase to my people.
The closest I would be able to come would be "a big wide river".
Am I then to tell my people that they are to be thrown into the big, wide river of the United States?

Earl Old Person
Blackfeet Tribal Chairman

Introduction

In the midst of twenty-first–century North America, how do the very first North Americans hold on to their unique cultural identity? At the same time, how do they adjust to the real demands of the modern world? Earl Old Person's quote on the opposite page expresses the difficulty of achieving this balance. Even the common values of the rest of North America—like fitting into the "mainstream"—may seem strange or undesireable to North American Indians. How can these groups of people thrive and prosper in the twenty-first century without losing their traditions, the ways of thinking and living that have been handed down to them by their ancestors? How can they keep from drowning in North America's "big, wide river"?

Thoughts from the Series Consultant

Each of the books in this series was written with the help of Native scholars and tribal leaders from the particular tribe. Based on oral histories as well as written documents, these books describe the current strategies of each Native nation to develop its economy while maintaining strong ties with its culture. As a result, you may find that these books read far differently from other books about Native Americans.

Over the past centuries, Native groups have faced increasing pressure to conform to the wishes of the governments that took their lands. Often brutally inhumane methods were implemented to change Native social systems. These books describe the ways that Native groups refused to be passive recipients of change, even in the face of these past atrocities. Heroic individuals worked to fit external changes into local conditions. This struggle continues today.

The legacy of the past still haunts the psyche of both Native and non-Native people of North America; hopefully, these books will help correct some misunderstandings. And even with the difficulties encountered

7

by past and current Native leaders, Native nations continue to thrive. As this series illustrates, Native populations continue to increase—and they have clearly persevered against incredible odds. North American culture's big, wide river may be deep and cold—but Native Americans are good swimmers!

—Martha McCollough

Breaking Stereotypes

One way that some North Americans may "drown" Native culture is by using stereotypes to think about North American Indians. When we use stereotypes to think about a group of people, we assume things about them because of their race or cultural group. Instead of taking time to understand individual differences and situations, we lump together everyone in a certain group. In reality, though, every person is different. More than two million Native people live in North America, and they are as **diverse** as any other group. Each one is unique.

Even if we try hard to avoid stereotypes, however, it isn't always easy to know what words to use. Should we call the people who are native to North America Native Americans—or American Indians—or just Indians?

The word "Indian" probably comes from a mistake—when Christopher Columbus arrived in the New World, he thought he had reached India, so he called the people he found there Indians. Some people feel it doesn't make much sense to call Native Americans "Indians." (Suppose Columbus had thought he landed in China instead of India; would we today call Native people "Chinese"?) Other scholars disagree; for example, Russell Means, Native politician and activist, claims that the word "Indian" comes from Columbus saying the native people were *en Dios*—"in God," or naturally spiritual.

Many Canadians use the term "First Nations" to refer to the Native peoples who live there, and people in the United States usually speak of Native Americans. Most Native people we talked to while we were writing these books prefer the simple term "Indian"—or they would rather use the names of their tribes. (We have used the term "North American Indians" for our series to distinguish this group of people from the inhabitants of India.)

Even the definition of what makes a person "Indian" varies. The U.S. government recognizes certain groups as tribal nations (almost 500 in all). Each nation then decides how it will enroll people as members of that tribe. Tribes may require a particular amount of Indian blood, tribal membership of the father or the mother, or other *criteria*. Some enrolled tribal members who are legally "Indian" may not look Native at all; many have blond hair and blue eyes and others have clearly African features. At the same time, there are thousands of Native people whose tribes have not yet been officially recognized by the government.

We have done our best to write books that are as free from stereotypes as possible. But you as the reader also play a part. After reading one of these books, we hope you won't think: "The Cheyenne are all like this" or "Iroquois are all like that." Each person in this world is unique, whatever their culture. Stereotypes shut people's minds—but these books are intended to open your mind. North American Indians today have much wisdom and beauty to offer.

Some people consider American Indians to be a historical topic only, but Indians today are living, contributing members of North American society. The contributions of the various Indian cultures enrich our world—and North America would be a very different place without the Native people who live there. May they never be lost in North America's "big, wide river"!

In the beginning, there was only water and sky. A woman fell from the world above, and great birds swept forth to catch her.

Chapter 1

Creation

In the beginning, this world was only water and air. There were swimming things and flying things, but the walking things lived in a world beyond the sky. One day, the clouds parted. A hole opened up in the sky, and one of the walking things fell through.

Aataentsic, the woman from the sky, tumbled from the world above to the world of water and air below. Two great birds saw her falling. They knew that she was not a flying thing or a swimming thing and that she could not live for long in this world as it was, so they spread their wings and swept toward her. They caught her on their great backs to save her from the water and carried her while the animals discussed what should be done.

The animals knew that Sky Woman would need a dry place to walk and live, but there was no land between the water and the sky. Then the turtle had an idea. He turned to the mighty water creatures and said, "Swim to the bottom of the waters and bring up land." But the water was so deep and dense that the great creatures could not swim to the bottom. When they all had attempted and failed to penetrate the dark waters, they gathered around, wondering what could be done. Then, a tiny voice broke through their discussions. It was the little toad who spoke.

"I can swim to the bottom, and bring back the land," the toad said. The other creatures laughed for the toad was so small. They said the toad would not be able to carry the land in his little arms. But the toad knew the mighty creatures were wrong, so he dove down. He swam deep into the dark places where the water became dense. His little body slipped past where the large creatures could not go. It took all his strength to swim so deep, but he struggled until he came to the very bottom of this world. There, he swept the sand and silt into his mouth. Then he swam back toward the light.

When the toad's head popped back up through the water, the great

The toad brought soil from down below, and the animals spread the earth across the turtle's back.

Aataentsic gave birth to a daughter. Under her mother's and grandmother's care, the girl grew up safe and happy.

creatures laughed again, for they saw no land in the toad's tiny arms. The humble toad opened his mouth in the face of this laughter, and the creatures grew silent. They saw the land he carried and knew it was a great thing the toad had done. The turtle said, "Now spread what you have gathered on my back. We will make dry land for Sky Woman, and she can live on my shell." So the toad spread the soil on the turtle's shell and dove back to the bottom to bring more land.

Over and over again, the toad dove down through the waters to gather more soil, and when he was done, a great expanse of land rose up on the turtle's back. When all was ready, the birds set Aataentsic on her new land.

Many spirits and beings inhabited the new land that the animals had created, and when Sky Woman began to explore, she came upon a lodge. She went inside and found an old woman living there. She called the old woman Shutai, which means grandmother. Shutai looked at Sky Woman and said, "Granddaughter, you were pregnant when you fell down from the world above the sky. I know the old ways. Stay with me until you give birth to your child." So Sky Woman stayed with Shutai and soon gave birth to a baby girl.

The girl grew up happily with her mother and grandmother on the new land the animals had created, and soon she was a young woman. She was very beautiful, and the male spirits who inhabited the island were enchanted by her. The male spirits all wished to marry the young woman, but she did not know which one to choose, so she asked her wise mother, Aataentsic. Her mother said to choose the turtle spirit, and the turtle spirit came to the sleeping daughter's bed. He placed an arrow beside the young woman whom he loved. Later he came back to fetch the arrow. When she awoke, the young woman did not know that the turtle spirit had come, and he never appeared again. But soon she realized that she was pregnant.

The first child she gave birth to was Tsestah whose name means "Man of Fire." There was a second baby as well. His name was Tawiskaron meaning "Man of Flint," and he refused to be born the normal way. Instead he came up through his mother's body and emerged from beneath her arm. When her second baby was born this way, the young woman died.

Corn and maple trees were important to the early Hurons. They saw them as gifts from Tsestah, the Man of Fire.

When you read this creation story in other places you may find that Tsetsah, "Man of Fire," is often given different names. Among them are Yoskaha, Jouskeha, and Tijuskaa. Often, with stories that have been passed down through many generations, different versions will develop over time. In other versions of the story, Tsetsah tells his brother that his greatest fear is corn or beans rather than an Indian grass braid.

Tawiskaron's spirit traveled to the Northwest, a place of monotonous plains and forbidding mountains.

The Balance Between Good and Evil

Many European, Christian, and Euro-American interpretations of the Wendat creation story see Tsestah as representing good and Tawiskaron as representing evil. Wendat religion and culture, however, did not draw the types of distinctions between good and evil that Western and Christian cultures draw. For example, Christian religions have God and the Devil as opposing forces, but Wendat traditions did not believe in a "god" that was all good and a "devil" that was all bad. Instead, they believed that all creation had a natural balance and that both good and evil were not only present but necessary to create that balance. Things that were all good or all evil would be thought of as equally dangerous because they were not in balance.

Man of Fire and Man of Flint were very different from each other and ruled the land with opposite ideas. The People were coming to the land, and Tsestah wanted to make life easy for them on the island. Because he was the firstborn, Tsestah could make the first preparations of the land for the people. He looked around at the land and decided he would make the animals big and fat so that they would be easy to hunt. He made the bushes and vines abound with plump, juicy berries that were inviting and easy for the animals and people to pick. He made sweet syrup run through the maple trees. He decided that all rivers should flow in two directions so that the people would not have to paddle, no matter which direction their canoe was going.

Then it was Tawiskaron's turn to make preparations for the people. He looked about at what his brother Tsestah had done and scoffed. "What kind of life is this," he asked, "where people and animals lie around lazy and fat? Why should people live where everything is good and easy and never have to work?"

Tawiskaron looked at the rivers his brother had made and said, "Sometimes, the people will float along with the current, but sometimes they will have to paddle their canoes to get where they are going." Then he turned the rivers so they all flowed in one direction. Next he looked at the fat animals and said, "Why should the animals be so easy for the people to kill? Hunting the animals will take great courage and skill." Then he made the animals sleek and skittish. He looked at the plump, succulent berries that the animals and people would feast on and said, "The animals and people will have berries for their feasts, but the berries will be small and protected by thorns." He looked at the maple trees with sugary syrup coursing through their veins and laughed, "The people will have syrup, but they will have to perform great labor by drawing it out of the trees and boiling it un-

Many contemporary Huron people still perceive spiritual meaning in the natural world.

til the sugar is revealed." With that he turned all of the syrup to a thin, watery sap that barely tasted sweet.

As Tawiskaron continued to alter Tsestah's creations, Tsestah grew more and more angry until a fierce rage was burning within him. He turned to his brother and challenged him to a race to decide who would have power in the land. As they made preparations for the race, the brothers asked each other what they feared most. Tawiskaron was truthful and told his brother that his greatest fear was deer horns. Tsestah, however, lied to his brother and said the thing he feared most was a braid of Indian grass. Then Tsestah gathered as many deer horns as he could find and placed them all along the course of the race. Tawiskaron went to his grandmother, Aataentsic, and asked her to help him weave a long braid of Indian grass.

On the day of the race, the two brothers began the competition with earnest. Tawiskaron's heart soon pounded with fear, for all around him stood sharp deer antlers. Tsestah ran unafraid. When Tsestah began feeling tired, he picked up the Indian grass braid and ate it to keep up his strength. But Tawiskaron became exhausted and disoriented by his fear. He began running in all directions trying to escape the antlers. Then he tripped and fell, and the antlers cut through his body. Tawiskaron stumbled about, blood dripping from his wounds. Wherever his blood fell, it turned into flint on the ground. Then Tawiskaron died, and his spirit rose up and traveled to the Northwest, the place where he had made flat, treeless plains and tall, forbidding mountains.

This is how the People's island was made and why today living things dwell in the East and the spirits of the dead go to the West.

At Sainte-Marie among the Hurons, a young woman makes pottery by a fire as her ancestors did years ago. (Photograph courtesy of Sainte-Marie among the Hurons, Midland, Ontario, Canada.)

Chapter 2

History

Whﬗen you think of ancient times and civilizations, people like the Greeks and Egyptians may come to mind. Maybe you think of kings and queens and pharaohs, or mysterious *scrolls* hidden in dark tombs and *hieroglyphs* carved into stone walls. But often when we think of the rich history and grand civilizations of the past, we forget that long before there were kings and queens, before the Vikings took to the seas, before the Greeks built the *Colosseum* and the *Parthenon*, even before there were books or written words, people lived on Turtle Island. We will probably never know how many people once lived in these vast lands, but we do know that great civilizations with complex *economies*, intricate governments, and diverse cultures thrived in the *Western Hemisphere* for thousands of years before Columbus and other Europeans claimed this land as their own.

One of the groups of people who lived in the land that is now called North America long before Europeans came was the Wendat (pronounced *one-dot*). The word Wendat means "island dweller." Some historians believe the Wendat used this name for themselves because of their creation story, which describes how the land was created as an island floating on the back of a great turtle. Others believe that the name referred to the fact that the area of land on which they lived was surrounded on three sides by water. Furthermore, in the Iroquoian language family (of which the Wendat language is a part) the word root *wen* refers to the voice or spoken language. Therefore, the name Wendat may have also meant that the Wendat people were seen as spokespeople or leaders in the surrounding communities.

In the 1500s, the Wendat lived on the southeastern corner of Georgian Bay, which lies between Lake Huron and Lake Ontario in the present-day

The Wendat people lived on the southeastern tip of Georgian Bay. The entire region was well populated with native people and had many land and water trading routes long before the arrival of Europeans.

Canoes have always been vital to the Wendat economy. In centuries past, the Wendat people used canoes to traverse the many waterways where they lived and to transport goods for trade. Today, canoe making remains one of the most important businesses of the Huron-Wendat of Wendake.

Canadian province of Ontario. The Wendat called their home Wendake. When the French first came to this land, however, they gave the Wendat people the name Huron and called the land on which they lived Huronia. Today, you will most likely hear the name Huron used when referring to this group of people, but even hundreds of years later many people still feel that the word Huron is a *derogatory* term.

The Wendat people were not a tribe. They were actually a *confederacy* of five nations. The largest was the Attignawantan, or Bear Nation. The next was the Attigneenongnahac, or Cord Nation. Then there was the Arendahronon, or Rock Nation. The fourth nation, Tahontaenrat is often called the Deer Nation, but its name may have actually meant "place of white thorns or bushes" or "the white-eared people." The fifth nation was called Ataronchronon or "the nation beyond the intervening swamp." No one knows how many people lived in the Wendat confederacy before Europeans brought guns and diseases, but estimates range from twenty-five to forty thousand people.

People of the Wendat nations lived in towns that were built near rivers, lakes, or other waterways. Protective walls made of pine and cedar logs surrounded the towns. These walls had lookout posts where men could sit and keep watch for friendly visitors or suspicious strangers. The Wendat were *agriculturalists* and the women kept fields of crops such as corn, beans, and squash outside of the town walls. The other main source of food was fishing, and men used spears, nets, and hooks to fish in the nearby streams, rivers, and lakes. Men also hunted animals such as bear, deer, beaver, moose, and birds. Despite the many types of fish and game that the men hunted, the most important food for the people was the corn that the women grew.

Within the town walls were rows of longhouses. A longhouse was a tall, rectangular building about one hundred feet (about 30.5 meters) long and thirty feet (about 9 meters) wide. The longhouse was made of a log frame covered by sheets of bark. The roof was arched with a series of holes running down the center for smoke to escape. Inside the longhouse, a row of cooking fires stretched down the center of the building. Two families shared each fire. On the floors were mats woven from bark or

Today, you will find that people from many different Native traditions refer to North America as Turtle Island. This name comes from the creation story existing in many tribes that describes the earth as being created on the back of a turtle.

The Wendat people lived in longhouses that housed an average of forty people. This longhouse stands in the recreated Wendat village at Sainte-Marie among the Hurons in Midland, Ontario, Canada. (Photograph courtesy of Sainte-Marie among the Hurons, Midland, Ontario, Canada.)

corn husks for sitting or sleeping. There were wide shelves along the walls where people could sleep or store belongings. About ten families lived in each longhouse (an average of forty people), and larger towns might have forty longhouses.

Today many people in North America and around the world think that this continent was relatively unpopulated when Europeans arrived, but think for a moment about the population of the Wendat confederacy. Consider if the confederacy had twenty-five thousand people (the smallest estimate of the Wendat population) and there were forty people living in each longhouse; that would mean 625 longhouses would have been in this small area on the shores of Georgian Bay alone! If the Wendat had forty

The early Wendat economy was based on farming and hunting. While women farmed crops like corn, beans, and squash, men hunted animals like white-tailed dear, beaver, bear, and moose. When the men began hunting animals for the fur trade, however, these natural resources were quickly depleted.

thousand people, there would have been about one thousand longhouses. And the Wendat was only one of hundreds of groups of Native people living in North America when Europeans arrived.

In many history books, you will read that the Iroquois were the arch-enemies of the Wendat people. These books say that the Iroquois and Wendat were constantly at war, battling, stealing each other's women and children, and viciously torturing captured warriors to death. However, since all of the recorded history from this time was written by Europeans who had just arrived on the continent, who did not speak the languages of the people and did not know anything about the people's lives or customs, it is difficult to know how much of what was written was true, how much was based on misunderstandings and incorrect interpretations, and how much were just plain lies that were told to make it easier and more acceptable to take advantage of the people already living on this continent.

According to Georges E. Sioui, a Wendat scholar and author of *Huron/ Wendat: The Heritage of the Circle*, though the Wendat and Iroquois had conflicts prior to European arrival, the true wars and bloodshed between these people did not begin until the Europeans arrived. When the French made contact with the Wendat people in the 1600s, they wished to purchase furs from the Wendat people. There was a huge market for furs, especially beaver pelts, in Europe where the furs were used to make warm and often luxurious clothing. Long before the Europeans came, the Wendat people had been leaders in trade, traveling great distances by canoe to trade their corn and other goods to people in the north, west, and south. These established trade routes soon became busy and valuable aspects of the booming market in North American furs.

Since so many men were now concentrating on trading in furs, fewer men were left to hunt and fish. With so many women engaged in scraping and preparing the pelts for sale, fewer women were left to tend to the fields. With less effort being put toward harvesting and storing their own food, the Wendat were becoming completely dependent on the fur trade for their survival. Just as the Wendat were growing dependent on the fur trade, so too were their southeastern neighbors, the Iroquois. However, the Iroquois traded with the Dutch, who competed with the French in the European fur markets.

Even as tensions in the fur trade were stirring the rivalries between the Wendat and Iroquois, there were even greater hardships facing the Wendat and all Native American people. The one thing the Europeans brought to North America that was even deadlier than swords and guns was disease. In Europe, people were exposed to numerous diseases such as smallpox, dysentery, cholera, the common cold, and the flu. These diseases

---

The name Huron came from the French word *hure*, which meant "boar's head." The French gave this name to the Wendat people because the men would sometimes wear their hair cut short and standing up in a line down the center of their head, a style that is called a mohawk today. Wild boars have a strip of spiky hair running down the centers of their heads and backs.

You can visit authentic recreations of longhouses on the Web or in person at a historical site called Sainte-Marie Among the Hurons in Ontario, Canada. To have the experience of sleeping in a longhouse and eating traditional foods cooked as they were long ago, you can spend the night at the Land of the Rising Sun. This is a Native American Cultural Site located outside of Québec City in Québec, Canada. Native and non-Native people alike come to this place to spend a few days learning about what life was like for the Wendat and other Native people hundreds of years ago.

never existed in North America before the Europeans came, so the Native people had no *immunity*. Even Europeans who did not appear sick carried diseases that proved deadly to the Wendat and to all Native people. No one knows how many Native people lived in North and South America before Europeans came to these continents. What we do know is that the death toll from these European diseases was in the millions. In the Wendat community alone, more than half the population was killed in less than five years. By 1640, their population fell from more than twenty thousand people to less than ten thousand people. That means that between the years 1635 and 1640, at least five Wendat people died of disease every single day. Imagine what it would be like if every morning you woke up to hear that five more people in your town or city had died of unknown diseases. This was happening not only in Wendake but everywhere that Native people had come in contact with Europeans.

As the tribes became weaker from disease and had fewer people to hunt and grow food, they became even more dependent on trade with the Europeans. Tensions grew over the lands where fur-bearing animals lived and the waterways that were used for transporting these furs. When all the animals in the southern portions of the lands had been killed, the people looked to the northern lands for more furs. The Wendats controlled the northern trade routes, and soon the Iroquois began attacking the Wendats in an attempt to gain control of the fur trade. The Dutch armed the Iroquois with guns. Some of the Wendats who had converted to Christianity had been given guns by the French as well, but they were no match for the Dutch-armed Iroquois. Many of the Wendat people were killed. Many others, realizing that the confederacy was all but destroyed, chose to join the Iroquois tribes. About one thousand people joined the Onondaga Tribe of the Iroquois confederacy. Others joined the Seneca Tribe. Many other Wendat, however, did not want to join the Iroquois. In 1649, less than fifty years after trade with the French began, the remaining people of the devastated Wendat confederacy fled the land of Wendake.

The Wendat people remained determined in the face of overwhelming pressure, violence, and change.

Chapter 3

A Journey Lasting Two Hundred Years

In the face of diseases and the onslaught of Iroquois, the Wendat people scattered in all directions. The largest portion of Wendat people divided into two main groups. One group sought safety across the water and traveled to an island in Georgian Bay. The second group traveled south. In the coming years, the Wendat people would have many homes and be forced to move many times. It would be more than two hundred years before some of the people settled in what would become their permanent homes.

After only one year on the island, the Wendat people living in Georgian Bay were starving, and the Iroquois continued their attacks on the people. Many of these people had converted to Christianity, and the Jesuit missionaries who had converted them convinced the group to move to Québec. About three hundred people left the island with the missionaries. As they traveled, other *displaced* Wendat people joined them. When they arrived in Québec, the group had about four hundred people.

As European influence on the North American continent increased, many aspects of Wendat life changed. This picture shows men wearing a combination of traditional Wendat and contemporary European/American dress. Although this picture is of men in the 1930s, European goods and styles were already influencing Wendat culture back in the 1600s.

The Wendat in Québec were not safe for long. By 1656, they were being attacked again—this time by the Mohawk Tribe of the Iroquois confederacy. This group of Wendat felt they could no longer withstand the Iroquois attacks, so they negotiated a treaty in which they agreed to divide into two groups. One group would join the Mohawk Tribe, while the other group would join the Onondaga. Over time, the Mohawk Tribe adopted the Wendat people who had joined them. The Onondaga, however, attacked the group of Wendat who had joined them, killed all of the Wendat men, and took the women and children as captives. Over the years, however, these captives also became part of the Onondaga Tribe.

Not all of the Wendat people in Québec, however, joined with the Iroquois. Two hundred Wendat people resisted and continued to live in Québec. They lived and moved with the missionaries, traveling from place to place until, in 1697, they settled in a place called Jeune Lorette and continued their relations with the French people until 1763.

In the decade from 1754 to 1763, the British and French fought each other for control of lands in North America. Many of the Native people, including the Wendat, fought as allies of the French. Today, this war is often referred to as the French and Indian War. When the British won the war, they called their newly conquered land Canada.

The British gave the northern group of Wendat people a reservation of 1,352 acres (547 hectares) and later a reservation of 9,600 acres (3,887 hectares). In the mid-1800s, however, the British government began a campaign to dismantle tribal governments and communities in Canada. They divided the **communal** land of the reservations into small **allotments,** which would be owned by individual families. Owning land as individuals was an unknown way of life to the Wendat people who had always held all land in common as a tribe. Then, in 1876, the British government took away all reservations in exchange for the "right" to vote. The northern group of Wendat people had mixed with French missionaries and the French community for a long time. Now, without communal lands or a recognized tribal government, they began to live even more like the Europeans who had sought to conquer them.

The Trail of Tears

Today the Trail of Tears is a name that many people know. However, most people tend to associate the name with the journey the Cherokee Nation made to Indian Territory. This journey, however, was not only made by the Cherokee but by all Native American tribes still living east of the Mississippi River. Some of these tribes include the Wendat, Creek, Seminole, Cherokee, Choctaw, and Chickasaw nations.

The group of Wendat traveling south first settled with some neighboring tribes. In the next ten years, this group would move four times, settling first on Michilimackinac Island in the present-day state of Michigan, then moving to an island in Lake Michigan, next to the Black River in the present-day state of Wisconsin, and finally further west to the southern shores of Lake Superior.

This southern group of Wendat had approximately five hundred people when they arrived at Lake Superior. But even here they did not stay for long. Ten years later, the Iroquois, French, and some other tribes were making agreements to end the long years of fighting, so the Wendat people, hoping to also make peace and once again trade openly with the French, moved back to Michilimackinac Island.

In 1701, the remaining people of the southern Wendat band moved to a

The "Right" to Vote

The ability to vote is a vital part of having one's voice heard in a democratic society. However, for people in minority groups, the "right" to vote often seems like another empty promise from the people in the majority who control the government. Even if you have the right to vote, if you are in a minority group, there often aren't enough voters to get your representatives elected. The votes of minority groups, like Native Americans, are often overwhelmed by the votes of majority groups, like white North Americans. Without significant representation in the government, the minority group may be essentially no better off than they were before they had the right to vote. Today, more and more Native Americans are serving in public office and government positions. However, for a long time Native Americans all over North America have expressed frustration with a system that gives them the apparent right to vote, but often leaves them without leaders in the state, provincial, and federal governments.

The Wendat people spent many years fleeing violence, fighting for land, and struggling for their culture's survival. Over time, many traditional practices and skills were lost. Today, many people are committed to relearning the ways of the past and carrying them into the future. (Photograph courtesy of Sainte-Marie among the Hurons, Midland, Ontario, Canada.)

French trading post to establish what they thought would be a permanent home. This trading post was called Detroit. Here they began a period of relative peace and prosperity as they formed alliances with neighboring tribes and served as leaders in the trading business. For more than fifty years, their prosperity continued as they spread through the lands of present-day Michigan, Ohio, and even into Pennsylvania. But new conflicts were brewing that would bring unimagined changes to the Wendat and all

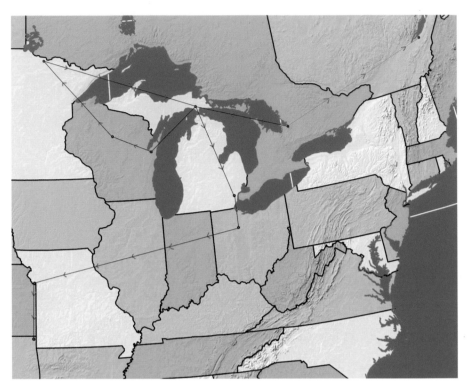

This map shows the long journey many of the Wendat people traveled after being forced from their ancestral home of Wendake. One branch journeyed northeast into Québec. Another branch spent two hundred years searching for a permanent home. In these years of struggle, Wendat people settled in many different places including Ontario, Québec, New York, Pennsylvania, Wisconsin, Minnesota, Michigan, Ohio, Missouri, Kansas, and Oklahoma.

of the Native people of North America. Once again, the Wendat way of life was about to change forever.

When the British won the French and Indian War, they took over the French trading routes. Many Native people wanted to continue fighting the British, but the Wendat Nation, now completely dependent on trade for the health of its economy and cut off from their French trading partners, were soon forced to establish trade with the British. The French had called the Wendat people "Huron," but the British used a variation of their native name, calling them "Wyandot." Today, the descendents of the Wendat people in the United States still call themselves Wyandot or Wyandotte.

Earlier in the eighteenth century, the Wyandots had control of land extending across present-day Ohio, present-day Michigan, and into present-day Canada, but British settlers were encroaching on these lands. After winning the Revolutionary War against the British in 1783, the settlers in the east began pouring into the Wyandot lands at a new pace. As the young country of America tried to expand its land holdings—and as the British tried to hold onto the land to which they still laid claim—the Wyandot people were forced to sign numerous treaties that traded their land for land in other places. Whenever one of these treaties was signed, the Wyandot found that the land they had been promised was also soon taken away or stolen by settlers who did not care what the treaties said. When the Wyandots tried to resist the stealing of their land, President George Washington sent the U.S. military to seize the land and to massacre anyone who resisted.

By 1805, the Wyandot people had lost nearly all their land. In 1830, the U.S. Congress passed the *infamous* Indian Removal Act. This law required all Native people living east of the Mississippi River to move to "Indian Territory," land in the present-day states of Oklahoma, Kansas, and Nebraska. Tens of thousands of people made the one-thousand-mile (1,700-kilometer) journey that today is referred to as the "Trail of Tears." For

---

A Testament to Where They've Been

When you travel through Québec, Ontario, Ohio, Michigan, Wisconsin, Kansas, Oklahoma, Pennsylvania, and elsewhere, you will find many places named after the Wendat Tribe and Wendat people. For example, Kansas City was once called Wyandot City, and many of its streets still bear the names of Wyandot families who lived there. Pennsylvania has Wyandot Falls, and Ohio has a Wyandot County and is even home to the Wyandot Popcorn Museum.

months, people traveled by foot, many of them without shoes, all of them with almost nothing to eat. Soldiers often killed the sick and the slow, or just left them behind to die alone while their families were forced to continue. Parents had to carry the children who were too young to walk, or the children also would die. Much of the journey was made in the winter months when frostbite, sickness, and starvation took their massive toll. Many thousands of those who began this journey never saw Indian Territory. Today, American homes, highways, parks, schools, and businesses are built on the unmarked graves of these people.

Many groups, including the Wyandot, tried to resist the removal to Indian Territory, but by 1843 the seven hundred Wyandots living in the United States were also forced to make the journey. When they arrived in Indian Territory, they were not given the 200,000 acres (80,972 hectares) of land the federal government had promised them. Instead, they had to purchase a 25,260-acre (10,227-hectare) parcel of land in Kansas from a tribe already living there.

Even on the new lands they had purchased in Kansas, the Wyandot people were not safe from the land lust of the American settlers. Soon, settlers were pouring into Indian Territory and claiming the land there as their own. Then the U.S. government began seizing the land in Indian Territory as well. According to new rules, the only land that was considered Indian Territory was now in present-day Oklahoma. The lands in Kansas and Nebraska were officially opened to settlers.

Over the next ten years, most of the Wyandots living in Kansas moved onto land in the northeastern corner of Oklahoma. In 1887, the U.S. government decided that the best way to deal with the "problem" of the Indian nations would be to take away all tribal lands and give the land to individuals. Such an arrangement was in the best interest of the U.S. government because when tribal lands were sold, the whole tribe had to agree to the sale and a treaty had to be approved by the tribal and federal governments. If individuals owned the land, those individuals could sell the land without the tribe's approval. The Dawes Act was passed, calling for all Indian lands to be divided and parceled out in 160-acre (65-hectare) allotments to individual families.

At the same time that the government was dividing the land among the Indians in Oklahoma, they were opening up all unclaimed land to settlers in what is now called "The Great Land Rush." Additionally, in 1891, President Benjamin Harrison ordered that 900,000 acres (36,437 hectares) of

Even after settling in Oklahoma, the Wendat people still were not safe from those who wished to steal their land. Oil speculators quickly bought much of the land out from under the tribes who had been forced into Indian Territory. Today, hundreds of oil wells pepper the entire state of Oklahoma. Every one of these oil wells stands on land that was promised to the Native American people.

the Indian lands of Oklahoma be opened to settlers. Many of the Indians who received land under the Dawes Act were in such desperate poverty that they were forced to sell their land in order to have money to survive. By the time land allotments were complete in Oklahoma, a book had been published showing the land allotments and giving the names of the people who owned them. The existence of this book made it easy for **oil speculators** to see who owned which land and where to go to buy it.

Assimilation into the white North American culture had always been a threat to the Wyandot people and to Native Americans in general, but the poverty the people faced in Oklahoma and the loss of tribal lands made that threat even more severe. Soon, with their population reduced from

Greyeyes Farewell Speech, Chief Bearskin, 1842

Adieu to the grave where my fathers now rest,
For I must be going afar to the west.
I have sold my possessions, my heart's filled with woe,
And now I must leave all, alas! I must go.

Farewell to the scenes that bind me like chains,
When on my gay pony I've pranced o'er the range.
The deer and the turkey I've traced in the snow;
But now I must leave all; alas! I must go.

Tymoctee, Sandusky and Broken-sword streams,
I no longer shall see thee, except in my dreams.
Adieu to the marshes, where cranberries grow.
To the great Mississippi, alas! I must go.

Farewell to the place where the cataract plays,
Where oft I have sported in my boyish days;
My dog and my hatchet, my arrow and bow
Were then my companions. Alas! I must go.

Adieu to the path that for many a year
I've traveled each Sabbath the Gospel to hear,
The words were so joyful and delighted me so,
From whence I heard them it pleased me to go.

Farewell to my white friends who taught me to pray,
To worship my Maker and serve Him each day.
Pray for the poor Indian whose eyes overflow,
With tears at our parting. Good-bye—I must go.

between twenty-five and forty thousand people down to just a couple hundred people, and all but the smallest pieces of land taken away, the original people of the Wendat confederacy were nearly unrecognizable as a tribe.

Recent decades have seen a type of *renaissance* occurring in native communities all over North America. Communities that survived the federal government's attempts to dissolve the tribes have pulled together and fought to once more have their communities and tribal governments recognized. Many tribes have been able to reinstate tribal chiefs and councils as well as reclaim parts of their reservations. With new economic prosperity, many tribes have been able to purchase land to add to these reservations.

The Wendat people have benefited in these recent decades as well. After having the remains of the confederacy scattered throughout North America, groups of Wendat/Wyandotte have joined together as tribal communities once more and are now working to regain some of what they have lost and reestablish a way of life uniquely informed by their Wendat heritage.

Though descendents of the Wendat confederacy now live all across the United States and Canada, four main communities survive. They are the Huron-Wendat of Wendake, the Wyandotte Nation of Oklahoma, the Wyandot Nation of Kansas, and the Wyandotte Band of Anderdon. Unfortunately, only the Huron-Wendat of Wendake and the Wyandotte Nation of Oklahoma are currently recognized as Indian tribes by the federal governments of Canada and the United States. Nevertheless, in 1999, leaders from all four groups met in Ontario, Canada, to reaffirm the Wendat confederacy.

The symbol of the Wyandotte Nation of Oklahoma graces the entrance of the nation's government building. The symbol features the nation's colors—red, black, and white. The twelve points on the turtle's back represent the twelve clans of the confederacy. The points surround the council fire, and the turtle holds a peace pipe and a war club in its forepaws. The willow branches that hang above the turtle's head symbolize the eternity of the people.

Chapter 4

Government
Past and Present

Long, long ago, before the Hawk Clan and before memory, there was a young woman who was too proud to live among her clan. The young woman left her people and went to live with her old grandmother deep in the woods.

Far away, on a tall mountain in the clouds, the great Bird King had slain his wife and thrown her body off the peak. Now there was no one to care for his two babies while he was hunting. He needed a wife to watch his nest.

One day, as the young woman was alone in the forest gathering berries, a great darkness came over the sky. She looked up. Above her, the king of all birds of prey spread his wings. His wings reached so far across the sky that they blocked the sun. The young woman was very frightened of the great Bird King, so she ran and looked for a place to hide from his piercing eyes. She saw a hollow log and dove into it, thinking she would be safe there.

The Bird King saw the young woman dive into the hollow log. He knew she was alone, far from her clan. He swept down, cutting the air with his wings, and seized the log in his mighty talons. Then he rose up from the forest floor and carried the log toward the sun.

When the Bird King set the log on the top of the great mountain, the woman crawled out very frightened. But when she emerged from the log, she saw a very strong and handsome man. The Bird King had turned himself into the form of a man so the young woman would live with him, and for a time she was happy and cared for the two birds in the nest. Even though they were just babies, they were already bigger than the young woman.

Then the young woman learned how the Bird King's first wife had died. She grew very frightened and knew she had to escape from the mountain. When the Bird King returned every evening in man form, the woman pretended nothing was wrong, but she was forming a plan. She chose the

Wendat society is matrilineal. Children become members of their mother's clan. (Photograph courtesy of Sainte-Marie among the Hurons, Midland, Ontario, Canada.)

larger of the baby birds and began feeding it extra pieces of the deer and elk that the Bird King brought back in his talons every day.

With the extra meat the young woman fed to him, the baby bird grew very large very fast. Then, when his feathers had sprouted, she lured him out of the nest and to the side of the mountain. With a mighty shove, she pushed the unsteady bird over the edge of the cliff and clung to his feathers as he clumsily flapped to the ground. She heard the Bird King's angry cry in the distance, so she quickly plucked the feathers from the young bird's wings so that he would not be able to follow her. Then she ran off into the forest.

The Bird King was filled with rage and searched for the young woman, but could not find her. Then he saw his crippled son lying on the ground and scooped him up in his claws. He flew back to the mountain and returned his son to the nest to heal. Meanwhile, the young woman returned to her grandmother in the forest. Soon, the young woman gave birth to hawk children, and she gave each of the children one of the feathers she had taken from the young bird's wings.

This is how the Hawk Clan came to be.

This is the traditional story of the creation of the Hawk Clan. In the past, the basic social and political structure of the people of the Wendat confederacy was the clan. Clans were very large, extended families. In North American society today, we think of our relatives as grandparents, aunts, uncles, cousins, and so on. The Wendat clan system, however, was very different. For example, no distinction was made between brothers and sisters and their cousins. Instead, all the children within a clan were considered to be brothers and sisters of each other. Because everyone in a clan was seen as a family member, people were forbidden to marry within their own clan. When a child was born, it became a member of the mother's clan. This type of society, where membership is passed down through the women of the family, is called a matrilineal society.

According to Wendat scholar, Georges E. Sioui, the Wendat confederacy had eight clans. They were the Turtle, Wolf, Bear, Beaver, Deer, Hawk, Porcupine, and Snake clans. According to some accounts, the Porcupine and Snake clans may have originally been the Loon and Fox clans. Each town had members from every clan living within it. The towns of the Wendat confederacy remained strongly united because clans in one town had clan family members in every other town. Marriages also made the

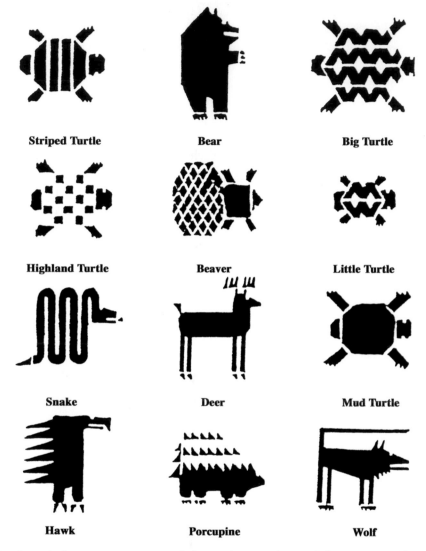

Striped Turtle	Bear	Big Turtle
Highland Turtle	Beaver	Little Turtle
Snake	Deer	Mud Turtle
Hawk	Porcupine	Wolf

Wendat scholar, Georges E. Sioui believes the Wendat confederacy originally consisted of eight clans. Historians of the Wyandotte Nation of Oklahoma, however, believe there were twelve clans. These are the symbols of the twelve clans. Millions of native people died when Europeans came to North and South America; because so many lives and so much history was lost, we will probably never know exactly how many people, tribes, or clans existed on these continents before Europeans arrived.

confederacy strong. Because you had to marry someone from a different clan, all of the clans became related to each other through marriage.

Though the clans were the **fundamental** social and political bodies of the Wendat people, the government actually existed on four different levels: the clan, the town, the nation, and the confederacy. Each clan within a town chose two leaders called chiefs. Chiefs were never considered to have power over other people. Rather, the chiefs were representatives who spoke for the people. Thus the chiefs were chosen for their ability to listen, discuss, accurately convey the people's wishes, and **diplomatically** resolve conflicts to the satisfaction of all members of the clan. The old women of the clan usually chose the clan's chiefs. If the chief was not serving the clan well, the women could dismiss him and choose a new chief.

The clans had two types of chiefs, a **civil** chief and a defense chief. The civil chief dealt with all matters of daily life, such as overseeing food distribution, ceremonies and celebrations, and resolving disputes. There was also a defense chief, who was in charge of matters of war.

All the clans within a town also came together to form a town council that served as the government of the town as a whole. All the civil and de-

A sign bearing the nation's symbol welcomes you to the tribal headquarters of the Wyandotte Nation of Oklahoma.

fense chiefs of the clans as well as the town *elders* sat on the council. The council would decide matters involving the whole town and would meet as often as every day if the situation required. The clans decided most matters of justice, such as punishment for crimes. If the clans could not settle a judicial matter or dispute, however, they would bring the matter before the town council.

Everyone who lived in the town was welcome to come and speak at council meetings. In all levels of Wendat government, a decision had to be *unanimous* before the people could take action. This was a truly *democratic* form of government in which every person had a voice. The entire system of government was based on listening, understanding, and compromise. People were encouraged to be open to others' opinions because they knew that a *consensus* would have to be reached before action could be taken. In town councils, the civil chief or chiefs who stood out as being particularly good representatives of the people would go on to represent the whole town in the third level of government.

The third level of the government was the nation. As we discussed earlier, there were five nations making up the Wendat confederacy. Civil chiefs representing the towns of each nation came together to form national councils. These national councils met to decide matters that would affect the whole nation. Such matters might include issues concerning trade routes or relations with the other nations. The most **distinguished** chiefs of the national councils then represented the nations at councils of the confederacy. The confederacy council met to discuss very large matters affecting all the nations, but they rarely handed down judgments on these matters. Because there were thousands of people involved at the confederacy level, it was very difficult to get everyone to agree on an issue. Therefore, a council meeting of the confederacy would usually be a time for all of the nations to meet, learn what was happening in the other nations, and discuss the challenges being faced. Then the individual nations would usually return with what they had learned and make their own decisions about what actions should be taken.

In the past, chiefs were important leaders of the Wendat people, and they remain important leaders today. This photograph is of Chief Philip Peacock who served as the principal chief of the Wyandotte Nation of Oklahoma from 1978 to 1983.

The Wyandot Council meets in this room at the Wyandotte Nation headquarters to discuss important matters concerning the tribe.

Today, the tribes that descended from the original Wendat confederacy have governments that mix aspects of the old tribal governments with newer forms of government that have been developed to deal with the specific needs of the people.

In the 1800s, the American and British governments dissolved the reservations and governments of the North American Indian tribes. In the twentieth century, however, the American and Canadian governments were forced to again recognize the tribes they had tried to obliterate, acknowledging their tribal governments and returning some reservation lands to the tribes. Today, approximately 2,500 descendents of the northern group of Wendat make up the Huron-Wendat of Wendake. More than one thousand members of the Huron-Wendat of Wendake live on the Wendake reservation, a 165-acre (approximately 67-hectare) area outside of Québec City, Québec. The remaining 1,500 members live throughout Canada.

Similar to times past, the Huron-Wendat of Wendake have a national council. Today, however, that council consists of five people who are elected by the members of the nation. Each council member is elected for a two-year term, and one council member is chosen as the chief councilor or Grand Chief. The chief councilor's position is similar to that of a chairperson in that the chief councilor's main responsibility is to oversee the council meetings.

The descendents of the Wendat group that traveled south now live throughout the United States, and many of them are members of the Wyandotte Nation of Oklahoma. Although a federally recognized tribe, the Wyandotte Nation of Oklahoma was never given reservation land. Instead, the tribe has purchased approximately 188 acres (about 76 hectares) of land where they settled in the northeastern corner of Oklahoma. Today there are approximately four thousand members of the Wyandotte Nation of Oklahoma, with about four hundred living within the tribal service area.

The Wyandot Council is the main governing body of the Wyandotte Nation of Oklahoma. The community elects a chief, second chief, and four councilors to this council. They are elected for two-year terms and a large part of their work consists of overseeing how money from the federal government and from tribal businesses is spent within the tribe. All members of the community are able to attend meetings with the council to express concerns and have their voices heard. These community meetings are held once each month.

The Wyandotte Nation of Oklahoma strives to provide many important services to its tribal members. A well-equipped fitness facility promotes good health. Use of this facility is free to tribal members.

Chapter 5

Economic Opportunities and Social Services

In the early 1900s, many members of the northern group of Wendat people found that they could make a living by making and selling their *traditional* arts and clothing. The most profitable of these arts have been snowshoe and canoe making. For many years, the Huron-Wendat of Wendake have been selling approximately three thousand canoes and fifty thousand snowshoes per year. Today, the Huron-Wendat of Wendake have expanded their traditional arts into such profitable businesses that they now enjoy one of the highest standards of living of all native people in Canada.

The Wendake reserve outside of Québec City consists of neighborhoods of homes, businesses, and tree-lined streets. Many people work in the shops and other businesses in the community. Artisans make crafts for

Many members of the Huron-Wendat of Wendake work in downtown Québec City in Québec, Canada. Many other tribal members work in businesses on the reservation, which is located just outside of the city. Here, the Huron-Wendat of Wendake run many economically prosperous businesses and enjoy one of the highest standards of living of any native groups in Canada today.

shops like Artisanat Gros-Louis (which sells everything from jewelry and peace pipes to showshoes and leather clothing), Les Produits Autochtones Terre de L'Aigle (Earth Eagle Native Products, selling incense, books, music, and snowshoes), and Huron Moc ENR (which sells handmade moccasins). There is a bookbinding store called Reliure Huronne where Ms. Francine Gros-Louis has been binding books for more than fifteen years. The Sagamité Restaurant features a blend of native, Canadian, and international cuisine. The Internet has also provided a great economic opportunity for the Huron-Wendat of Wendake. With the Internet, business owners can advertise and sell products to more people in more places all over the world.

In addition to the people employed in the thriving businesses of Wendake, many other people work in non-tribal jobs in downtown Québec City and elsewhere. Members of the Huron-Wendat of Wendake work in numerous fields such as being doctors, professors, authors, and *activists*.

The Huron-Wendat of Wendake do not only provide economic opportunities to the community, but social programs as well. Indian and Northern

The Turtle Stop is a combination gas station and convenience store. It was the Wyandotte Nation of Oklahoma's first economic development project.

WYANDOTTE NET TEL

Wyandotte Net Tel trains people for employment in computer networking, secretarial work, and technical writing. The Wyandotte Nation of Oklahoma is one of the largest employers in the area.

Affairs Canada is the name of the department responsible for federal money and programs for *First Nations* peoples. Money generated within the tribe and money from the Canadian federal government goes to providing health care, housing, and educational opportunities to community members. Health Canada, the federal health department, offers programs such as Aboriginal Diabetes Initiative, Fetal Alcohol Syndrome/Fetal Alcohol Effects, Injury Prevention and Control, and the National Native Alcohol and Drug Abuse Program to Native communities. Health Canada also runs the First Nations Head Start on Reserve program to prepare young children for entering and succeeding in school. In Wendake, children from first to fourth grade attend the Huron Elementary School. They continue their education in public schools in nearby Loretteville and Québec City.

The Wyandotte Nation of Oklahoma is one of the largest employers in its area. There are eight different tribes located in the northeastern corner of

Oklahoma, and together they are the dominant economic provider for this section of the state. The Wyandotte Nation alone runs a number of businesses that are very important to the Native and non-Native communities.

The Turtle Stop, built in 1987–1988, was the first economic development project of the Wyandotte Nation of Oklahoma. Although it is no longer the largest economic provider for the Nation, the Turtle Stop's gas station and convenience store remain not only as valuable resources for the tribe but as symbols of the Wyandotte Nation's growth, advancement, and commitment to independence.

Some of the most important economic providers for the tribe are the educational institutions that it runs. The Wyandotte Nation of Oklahoma has opened five technical schools where people train in fields such as paralegal, court reporting, and medical transcription. The Nation currently has schools in Oklahoma City, Kansas City, Albuquerque, Tulsa, and Phoenix.

Wyandotte Network Communications and Wyandotte Net Tel are two more businesses owned by the tribe. Wyandotte Net Tel provides employment opportunities by training people to work in areas such as computer networking, secretarial work, and technical writing. Then Net Tel contracts these trained workers out to other companies.

The Nation is concerned as well with providing services. One of the biggest economic projects the tribe has is also one of the biggest providers of services. The Wyandotte Fitness Center and Clinic is the first project of a new ten-year plan that will provide increased social services and economic prosperity. The Fitness Center features equipment for cardiovascular workouts, weight training, an indoor track for walking and running, and special features like tanning beds. There is a personal trainer on staff at the center. There is also a kitchen for teaching people about proper diet and diabetic concerns. The facilities are free to tribal members and cost only twenty-five dollars per month for non-tribal families in the community. Between one hundred and one hundred twenty people use the Fitness Center every day.

The Bearskin Clinic is also a very important resource for the community. Here people have access to a doctor, nurse, lab-technician, and X-ray machine. The Bearskin Clinic services approximately sixteen people each day, but due to lack of funding and federal restrictions on their operations, it is not able to provide all the services that community members need. Currently, people living in the area must travel great distances to get health care services that the clinic can't provide. People with private health insur-

"Kill the Indian to Save the Child"

These words should make your blood run cold, but it was a sentiment still being heard all over North America as recently as fifty years ago. Today, many Native communities are able to run their own preschools, elementary, and even high schools. But this hasn't been the case for very long. If loss of land and tribal government hadn't been enough, Native parents in the United States and Canada then lost their children to federally sponsored and often "religiously" run Indian schools. In these boarding schools, Indian children literally had their heritage beaten out of them. When they were brought to the schools, they had their hair cut and their clothing taken away. They were dressed in school uniforms and punished severely if they spoke their Native language. Today, more than anything else, Indian boarding schools are to blame for the extensive, perhaps irreversible, loss of language that has occurred in tribes all over North America. If you visit the grounds of old Indian boarding schools today, you will often see graveyards on the schools' grounds where the hundreds of children who died in these institutions are buried.

ance are able to use this coverage to pay for their care, but those who do not have insurance and need care beyond what the clinic can provide will have that care paid for by the tribe.

In addition to the fitness facilities and clinic, the Wyandotte Nation also runs a senior citizen center where seniors gather daily for a nutritious lunch, activities, and socializing. The center serves lunch to about one hundred people every day and anyone from the community who is over fifty-five years old can eat there for free—even if they are not tribal members. The senior citizens also take trips together (recent trips included the Ice Capades and horse racing), have their own musical band, and hold dances on the second Thursday of every month.

Advancing education is very important to the Wyandotte people as well, and in the Wyandotte Nation of Oklahoma, they begin stressing education

This is the Wyandotte Nation's senior citizen facility. Senior citizens from the tribe and from the surrounding community gather here for nutritious meals and socialization.

at a young age. Children living in the service area of the Nation attend the Turtle Tots Learning Center, the highest ranked Indian preschool in the United States. The preschool has both a summer and winter program and has approximately thirty children from ages zero to five.

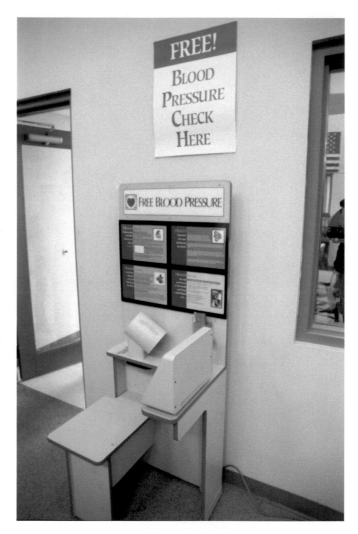

The Wyandotte Fitness Center and Clinic is part of a new ten-year plan to bring increased services and prosperity to the tribe. Within its walls, you can get a workout, relax in a hot tub, get your blood pressure checked, or take classes on good nutrition.

Kathy Deweese, the Wyandotte Nation's housing director, stands proudly beside a bulletin board displaying photographs of houses the tribe has built for its tribal members.

The Wyandotte Nation of Oklahoma Is very community minded, concentrating not only on the advancement of the tribal community but of all the people living in the area. Facilities such as the fitness and senior citizen centers and programs like the Turtle Tots are free to tribal members, but are also open to all members of the community. Currently, about half the children in Turtle Tots are tribal members while the other half are not tribal members.

The Wyandotte Nation Housing Authority plays a very important role in the Wyandotte, Oklahoma, community. This tribal department builds and renovates homes within a fifty-mile (85-kilometer) radius of the tribal headquarters. Since it began, the housing authority has built forty new houses, renovated forty existing houses, and dug forty new wells and septic tanks. The ownership program run through the housing authority gives many people the opportunity for home ownership. By setting low monthly payments of between $175 and $350 per month (depending on income) many people who otherwise could not afford it are able to buy their own homes.

Used in ceremonies, cornhusk masks like this one played an important role in Wendat spirituality.

Chapter 6

Oral Traditions and Spirituality

Stories, an important part of all peoples and cultures, are the foundations for understanding who we are. Stories abound all around us, making our lives rich with history, meaning, and even entertainment. But stories that seem like entertainment are often much more. They are a vital part of our existence. Stories are spiritual things, for they teach us about where we came from, why we are here, and how we should live in the world. Wherever you go in the world, whatever society or culture you visit, you will find stories, and the Wendat people are no exception.

Stories are often about beginnings. Every Native American tribe has a creation story that tells how the tribe began and how the earth, animals, and plants were created. The oral traditions of the tribes teach many other lessons as well. For example, many stories tell how cultural traditions, customs, practices, and beliefs began and why they are important. Here is a version of a story with important spiritual lessons from the Wendat oral tradition.

Once a Wendat man and his wife were traveling from their village to visit a village nearby. They went up the high mountain into the forest of tall pines. The lake shimmered below and the forest grew dark from the trees. They began descending toward the lake when suddenly a group of bears tumbled from the hill above and surrounded the man and woman.

The man and woman stood frozen with fear as the bears cut off all avenues of escape. They man and woman were sure they were about to have their flesh torn to pieces and their bones crunched. The leader of the bears stood up on his hind legs, but instead of tearing the man and woman to shreds, he spoke.

"Now you must come to our home in the Red Mountains. You will live there with us until we have decided you are ready to return to your people."

The man and woman knew that these must be very intelligent and powerful spirits who had taken the form of bears and that they should be greatly feared. They knew there was no choice but to go with their terrible companions. The man and woman held each other tightly and began the mysterious journey.

Soon it began to seem that there was no reason to fear the bears at all, for instead of being vicious and menacing they were jolly and *riotous*. They romped, rolled, tusseled, and played. There seemed to be no end to their games. To the man, they seemed just like village boys with their wrestling, shouting, and laughter. Soon the young man was infected by their mischievous behavior and also wished to join in the fun. He rollicked with the mighty bears, becoming bruised and battered by their paws and teeth, but bravely continuing in the play. The bears looked on the young man approvingly and gave each other wise smiles.

The sun was setting and the Red Mountains appeared on the horizon. The frolicking died down, the mood growing solemn. Once again, the leader of the bears stood and spoke.

"You have come to the Red Mountains, the sacred home of the Bears. Our grandfather's blood anoints these peaks. We have prepared a cave for you making it warm with dry leaves so you may sleep and be surrounded by the best nut-bearing trees so you may eat. There is no way for you to

The man and woman tried to escape the mountains, but the bears brought them back for they had to learn their medicine.

escape, so do not bend your minds to plotting and sorrow. Instead, find happiness and contentment in what we have provided for you here."

For a time the man and woman lived comfortably in their new home as they were directed, but soon they were visited by their memories and their hearts sang for their people. The man would not stay any longer and told his wife they must escape and return to their village.

Together the man and woman fled through the Red Mountains, but the bears soon overtook them. The bears turned to each other and said, "He who casts away kindness and runs from those who provide his house and food deserves death." They took him in their mighty paws and threw him down from the great mountain so that every bone in his body broke. Then they picked up his battered body and carried him back to the cave.

"All that we have done, we have done for the good of the people," the great bear told them. The Wendat people believed that all natural things, from bears to stones, had spirits and deserved respect.

The Wendat believed that the natural world was full of supernatural power.

With the man lying in agony in the cave, the bears turned to his wife and carefully described leaves, roots, and barks to her. They told her that if she wanted her husband to live, she must go alone into the forest and find the plants they had described. When she returned with everything they had asked for, the bears sat with her and taught her how to prepare the plants in a mixture that would make her husband well. When she did as the bears had instructed, her husband became well and whole again.

The agony he endured had little effect on the man's heart for the very next day he again tried to escape across the Red Mountains and again the bears pursued him. They said, "Once more he runs from us, the ones who give him a comfortable home and good meat to eat. Indeed he deserves death." So they tore the man's flesh with their sharp claws. Then they

Christian missions were built all over North America in an attempt to convert the native people of this continent to Christianity. Sainte-Marie among the Hurons was one of these missions. Today, however, it stands as a historic site with a recreated Wendat village. (Photograph courtesy of Sainte-Marie among the Hurons, Midland, Ontario, Canada.)

brought the man back to his wife in the cave, and showed her what plants to gather and how to make the medicine to dress his wounds. When she had done all that they had instructed, the man was again healed.

Day after day they continued like this, the man running from the bears and the bears pursuing and punishing him. Each time he fled, the bears returned him to his wife with a new affliction. One day the bears would give him a disease, another day a new injury. And each time they returned him in his pathetic state, they taught his wife how to cure his affliction.

Then one day after all of this had gone on for a long time, the bears came to the man and woman, and for the last time they spoke.

"All that we have done, we have done for the good of the Wendat people. We are friends of the people and as such we have made you ill and given you injuries and taught your wife to heal all that harmed you. Now

Sainte-Marie among the Hurons was built in 1639 in the Wendat land of Wendake. Here, Jesuit missionaries sought to convert the Wendat people to Christianity. Today, workers at the historic site focus on recreating the past and making the old traditions part of the present. (Photograph courtesy of Sainte-Marie among the Hurons, Midland, Ontario, Canada.)

she alone knows the powerful medicines that will heal the people's afflictions. You have learned all that we desired to teach you. Now take what you have learned back to your home, which your hearts have been longing for, and teach it to the people. Tell the people how the bears helped you. Tell them to never dishonor the bones of the bears they kill for food, and warn them to never let the names of the Bear Clan die."

The man and woman left the Red Mountains and returned to their people. From that day forward, the Wendats had medicine to heal all of their ills.

This is how medicine came to the Wendat people.

The story of how the bears gave medicine to the Wendat people shows a number of important aspects of Wendat spirituality. When the man and woman are surrounded by the bears, they realize that these are actually

A picture of the Old Wyandot Mission Church in Upper Sandusky, Ohio. Like so much of their land and heritage, the Wendat people had to leave this church behind as they were forced to move to Indian Territory.

powerful spirits who have taken bear form. The Wendat people believed that all natural things, from living creatures like humans, plants, and animals, to seemingly *inanimate* things like rocks, water, and air, had okis. An oki could be thought of as a spirit, soul, or supernatural power. Powerful okis could take the shapes of different things or inhabit different forms. The Wendat saw themselves as being surrounded by the spirits of the world all the time, and these spirits could both help and harm the people.

Each Wendat town had a medicine man, a wise person with the ability to communicate with human and nonhuman oki, determine their desires, and learn from their wisdom. The story of how the Wendat people got medicine shows us that, unlike the way most North Americans think of medicine today, the Wendat people saw medicine as a very spiritual and holy thing. It was not the chemical properties of a plant, tea, or poultice that healed the body of a sick person. Rather it was the oki of the plant or other medicine that healed the person's oki and therefore the person's body as well. Just as in the creation myth in chapter one, which showed that the natural stability of creation came from having a balance between positive and negative forces, so too oki were seen as neither wholly good or wholly evil, but rather as powerful and dangerous if treated in the wrong way. Healing was a matter of bringing the sick soul back into the balance of nature.

Through the *holocaust* of disease and war that the Wendat people endured, not only were tens of thousands of lives lost, but many of the oral traditions and spiritual ways were lost or forgotten as well. Furthermore, some of the first Europeans the Wendat people had contact with were Christian missionaries.

The missionaries were the main source of the diseases that devastated the Wendat people. At this time, they could not help but notice that the people who spent the most time with the missionaries were the first ones to catch diseases and die, yet the missionaries themselves remained unaffected. Different people interpreted this in different ways. Some people believed that the missionaries were using witchcraft or other means to purposefully make the Wendat sick. This made many people extremely resistant to the missionaries. Other people thought that the missionaries' god must be protecting them from the diseases and that perhaps the diseases were even a punishment from this god for not believing in and obeying him. This made the missionaries' god seem very powerful, and so

The Wendat did not equate light and dark with good and evil. Instead, they believed that both light and dark were two necessary halves of a whole. An imbalance between the two was dangerous, however.

many people converted to the Christian faiths in hopes of being saved from the diseases.

Today, the Huron-Wendat of Wendake, having descended from the group of Wendat who traveled to Québec with the missionaries, are almost all Christians. The Catholic church, Nôtre-Dame-de-Lorette, has stood on the Wendake reserve outside of Québec City for hundreds of years and is still where many of the members of the tribe attend church today.

Many of the Wyandotte Nation of Oklahoma, the Wyandotte Band of Anderdon, the Wyandot Nation of Kansas, as well as other Wendat descendents all over North America, are also members of Christian faiths. But others prefer to practice a blend of Christian and traditional beliefs. Furthermore, recent decades have seen a movement in these communities and native communities all over the United States and Canada to rediscover and reclaim the spiritual traditions of the past even while practicing the beliefs that have become the traditions of the present.

Today, many non-Native people around the world have become very interested in Native American forms of spirituality. In many cases, this has led to a deeper understanding of and respect for these beliefs. But in other cases, it has led to people disrespecting the beliefs by doing things like performing ceremonies they know nothing about or selling spiritual objects as mementoes, trinkets, and collectables. Additionally, many non-Native people think they have a right to visit Native people's ceremonial grounds, watch the ceremonies, take pictures of what they see, and even participate in the dances. This is very hurtful to many Native people who feel that such visitors treat their sacred way of life like a tourist attraction. Many people forget that being permitted to see a person's private spiritual life is an incredible privilege and great honor and should always be treated with the utmost respect and appreciation.

A painting of Leaford Bearskin. Mr. Bearskin has been principal chief of the Wyandotte Nation of Oklahoma since 1983.

Chapter 7

Contributions

Today, some American citizens assume that democratic government is an idea that the European settlers in America came up with when they became dissatisfied with being ruled by a **monarchy**. Of course this is not true. Different versions of democratic governments were practiced all over the world for thousands of years before "America" was even a word, let alone a country with a government. Many native tribes of North America, like the tribes of the Wendat confederacy, practiced democratic governments, and when the young United States began forming its government, it modeled some of its aspects after features seen in the governments of the Native tribes.

When the U.S. government was first being formed, the settlers did not know exactly how they wanted their government to run. What they did know, however, was that they wanted to be able to make decisions for themselves without a person, such as a king or a queen, ruling over them, commanding them in what to do and taking the wealth that the people generated.

When Mr. Bearskin first became chief, the Wyandotte Nation had no tribal buildings. Today his office is located in the tribal headquarters, and a bigger government building and more community services are planned for the future.

One of the places the settlers looked when developing their new representative government was to the Native people. Native governments like those of the Wendat tribes had chiefs who served, not as rulers over, but as representatives of the people. Furthermore, the chiefs did not serve the communities alone. The chiefs sat on councils of other chiefs and elder advisors. Civil and defense matters were the responsibilities of different people, so everyone had to come together and discuss issues before decisions could be made. No one person had the power to make a decision and take action without the consent and approval of the people. Furthermore, all members of the community gathered together to voice their opinions in the making of important decisions. In Wendat society, it was not acceptable for larger or stronger clans in a community to overwhelm or disregard the opinions of smaller clans in the community. Many of the positive, democratic features and aims of our modern U.S. government were actually modeled after the democratic ideals displayed in governments of North American tribes like those that made up the Wendat confederacy.

The Native people of North America are one of the smallest and historically most oppressed groups in the population of North America. Never-

Chief Bearskin has made great contributions to his people and to the people of America. He is not, however, the only person working hard for the advancement of the Wyandotte Nation. Second Chief Jim Bland (left) has worked alongside Chief Bearskin for many years focusing on the economic development of the tribe. Tribal Historian, Juanita McQuistion (right) dedicates herself to preserving the nation's past.

theless, more Native Americans have served in the national armed forces of the United States and Canada than any other ethnic or cultural group. You may think that after all they have been through the Wyandotte people would no longer want anything to do with the United States, but this is not true. Many of the Wyandotte people (as well as most Native people) are fiercely patriotic and have been serving in the American military since before they were considered citizens of this country.

An example of a man who has served both the Wyandotte Nation of Oklahoma and the American nation as well is Chief Leaford Bearskin. Mr. Bearskin, born in 1921, has served as Chief of the Wyandotte Nation of Oklahoma since 1983 and has seen and *facilitated* many positive changes within the community in this time.

Chief Bearskin was born and raised on his parents' allotment of land in Oklahoma. He joined the military right after graduating from high school. After a few short years of training and assignments, he was flying a B-24 Liberator Bomber in World War II and flew forty-six combat missions as an Aircraft Commander. He was a member of the famous Jolly Rogers. In 1948, he flew twenty-nine missions as a Squadron Commander. In all the flights he made, his plane was never shot down, and with a record so good, many people wanted to ride with him.

Mr. Bearskin later served in numerous commanding positions in Georgia, Korea, and Nebraska. In 1960, with the rank of Lieutenant Colonel, Mr. Bearskin retired from the Air Force and began serving the United States in a new way: as Chief of Vehicle and Aerospace Ground Equipment at Vandenberg Air Force Base in California. Nine years later, his responsibilities increased as he moved on to another position in the *federal civil service*, this time as Executive Officer to the Director of Operations at the Fifteenth Air Force headquarters.

When most people retire after forty years of service to their country, they don't think of starting whole new careers, but only four years after he retired from the U.S. civil service, Mr. Bearskin began a new career serving his people. After forty years of serving and protecting the people of the United States, Mr. Bearskin dedicated himself to restoring and building a new life and government for the Wyandotte people. Since being elected as chief of the Wyandotte Nation of Oklahoma, Mr. Bearskin has played a central role in developing economic opportunities and social services for the community and giving the Wyandotte people a reason to enter the

This Amerindian home in Québec, Canada shows a mixing of traditional and contemporary styles. In his time as grand chief of the Huron-Wendat of Wendake, Max Gros-Louis saw his people rise to have one of the highest standards of living among all native groups in Canada. Under his leadership, many natively owned homes and businesses rose and prospered in Québec.

twenty-first century with pride in their accomplishments and hopes for the future.

Born in 1931 in Wendake, Québec, Grand Chief Max Gros-Louis has spent most of his life working tirelessly for the fair treatment, equal rights, and international respect not only of the Huron-Wendat of Wendake but for *aboriginal* people all over the world.

In his autobiography, *First among the Hurons*, Gros-Louis discusses how

The idea that all members of a community could discuss their concerns and had to reach an agreement before government actions could be taken must have seemed revolutionary to the Europeans of the time who were controlled by absolute rulers. The idea probably still seems revolutionary or even impossible to many people today. Imagine how difficult it is just to get every member of your own family to agree on something, let alone hundreds of people. However, people in the Wendat community were raised valuing and understanding the need for cooperation, and with these social values, they may have found it easier to agree and accept compromises than people living in North American society today.

he grew up with, but never accepted, the *prejudices* against his people. The school in Wendake only educated children through fourth grade, so Gros-Louis studied through ninth grade in the nearby town of Loretteville. Lack of opportunities for higher education did not stop him from pursuing further schooling. He continued to study on his own and through *correspondence programs*. He focused on studying laws specific to aboriginal communities, and then embarked on a career meant to change the national laws, ideas, and prejudices that defined native people's lives in Canada.

In 1964, Max Gros-Louis was elected Grand Chief of the Huron-Wendat of Wendake. He served in this position for twenty years, making huge advances, perhaps most notably in arts and economic opportunities for his community. He retired from this position in 1984, but three years later ran for reelection and remained as the Grand Chief of the Huron-Wendat of Wendake until 1994.

Besides his leadership within his own community, Gros-Louis has been a dedicated leader committed to *reaffirming* the cultures and rights of all Native people. To this end, he began and served within numerous organizations. He has served as the director of the Assembly of First Nations, the administrator of the Aboriginal Economic Development Program, a founder of the Association des Indiens du Québec, director of the World Assembly of First Nations, and served on numerous other councils.

In his lifetime, Gros-Louis has received much respect and many awards for the work he has done and the influence he has had in areas of art, cultural heritage, economic development, and government recognition for the Huron-Wendat of Wendake and the First Nations peoples of Canada. Thought of as an elder in his own and many other Native communities, the work Max Gros-Louis and others like him do for their own communities ultimately aids in the restoration and advancement of oppressed cultures around the world.

In the past, the Wendat people strove to live in harmony with the natural environment. Today, the ancestors of these people realize that the natural world is in jeopardy. Renie, a miniature, talking version of a recycling truck, travels with his creators to schools in Oklahoma and the surrounding states. Barbara Collier, Environmental Director for the Wyandotte Nation, designed Renie to teach children the importance of recycling. Renie stands for Recyclable Education Needs in the Environment.

Chapter 8

Challenges of Today, Hopes for the Future

One of the biggest challenges facing the descendents of the Wendat people today is the loss of their original language and the desperate attempt to rediscover the language before all memory of it has disappeared. Although some individuals of the Wyandotte Nation of Oklahoma, such as Chief Bearskin, and of the Huron-Wendat of Wendake still know some elements of the language that was handed down from their ancestors, there are no longer any fluent speakers of the language.

In the future, through careful documentation and research of old historical records, many Wyandotte people hope to be able to reclaim the language that has been lost. Furthermore, as evidenced by meetings between the Huron-Wendat of Wendake, the Wyandotte Nation of Oklahoma, the Wyandot Nation of Kansas, and the Wyandotte Band of Anderdon, the Wyandotte people would like to restore the Wendat confederacy and in-

Educating their young people is very important to the Huron-Wendat and Wyandotte people. This library is located at the Wyandotte Nation tribal headquarters and is open for the public's use.

crease communication between all communities descended from the Wendat people. One challenge facing the people as they try to reestablish the confederacy is that, when the Wendat originally split, they joined distinctly different cultural groups. Today, the Huron-Wendat of Wendake are French speaking and uniquely influenced by French culture while the Wendat descendents throughout the rest of North America are English speaking and influenced by American and English-Canadian culture.

Reestablishing the Wendat confederacy may seem like a large task, but for the Wyandot Nation of Kansas, just being recognized by the federal government as a tribe has been extremely difficult. Throughout the 1990s, the Wyandot Nation of Kansas has been petitioning the government for federal recognition. If they are able to gain this recognition, they will be entitled to the same rights of **sovereign** government, land ownership, economic development, and federal funding for health, housing, and social programs to which the other tribes have access.

Probably the most serious and frightening challenge currently facing the Wyandotte Nation of Oklahoma is an environmental threat affecting all the people living in the northeastern corner of the state. A private company once owned a lead and zinc mine in the area and a lot of the mine extended onto Indian property. The company has since abandoned the mine, but left a true environmental disaster in its wake. Lead, zinc, and many other pollutants from this mine are now infecting the soil and leaching into the water of the area. The Wyandotte Nation of Oklahoma is located near the shores of a beautiful lake and river. Three major waterways pass through the tribal lands, but pollutants like these in the waterways kill fish, birds, and **habitat,** and they move dangerously up the food chain. The waterways also carry the pollutants downstream to communities located below the

The effects of pollution from mining will be felt long into the future. The lead and zinc mine formerly operated in Wyandotte Nation territory poses an undeniable threat, not only to the health of the natural environment, but to the health of all the people living in the area.

The prosperity that gaming has brought to Native American communities has allowed some tribes in New York State to return their portion of federal funds to the federal government, allowing the tribes to become economically independent. Someday, the Wyandotte Nation of Oklahoma would like to enjoy similar independence.

mine. These metals and pollutants in people's drinking water cause mental retardation and even death. Most people in the area get their water from underground wells, and many wells have been polluted by the abandoned mine. Today, the tribe's environmental department tests the wells of both Native and non-Native people living in the area to see if the people's water is safe to drink. They are also beginning to check every new student for lead poisoning when the child enters school.

Although the tribal environmental department offers education and water testing for the community, and hopes to offer more help in the future, it simply does not have the resources to deal with this type of environmental disaster. A polluted site like the remains of this lead and zinc mine takes many millions of dollars to clean up. That is money that the tribal government does not have and that the federal government is not likely to give. Even if the site is someday cleaned up, the effects of the pollution will be felt well into the future.

Although the environment is currently a serious concern, there are also very positive and hopeful developments in the tribe's near future. As many other tribes have done, the Wyandotte people hope to enter into the business of "Indian gaming," a name given to the explosion of bingo halls and casinos on tribal lands.

In some ways, casinos and bingo halls are very controversial. The controversy tends to come from state officials and religious organizations that believe gambling is wrong or that it will attract crime. Within the Indian communities, however, people have seen how gaming has saved the tribes from desperate financial circumstances, allowing them to become more independent and to no longer rely entirely on the federal government for financial support. Native Americans have seen time and time again that the American government cannot always be relied upon to adequately address

Water pollution is a serious environmental challenge facing the Wyandotte Nation of Oklahoma.

In the next ten years, the Wyandotte Nation hopes to expand this fitness complex to include an auditorium where tribal meetings can be held and a swimming pool.

a tribe's needs, so every opportunity for independence is seized with enthusiasm. Most Indian nations feel that it is only through economic independence that they can gain true political independence.

Not everyone in the Wyandotte Nation, however, sees gaming as a long-term solution to the need for economic growth. Second Chief Jim Bland knows that gaming won't be able to support the tribe forever. He wants to develop economic opportunities and businesses that will support the tribe for many years, providing jobs and opportunities for advancement within those positions. Nevertheless, he thinks that the money gaming could bring in would be a very big help to the programs the tribal government is currently trying to expand. For example, currently the tribal government does not have enough money to provide the type of health care that its members need. If able to open halls for bingo and slot machines, they believe that in five years they will have enough money to run their health care programs. If they are not permitted by the state government to enter the gaming business, they fear it will take twenty-five years to make the planned improvements to the health care system.

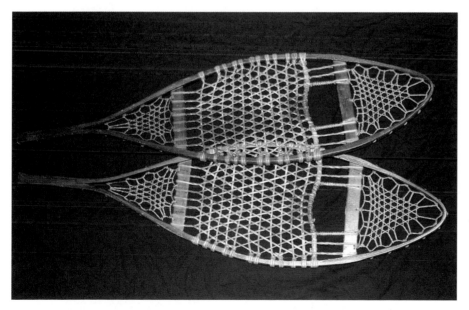

Many contemporary Huron-Wendat of Wendake still make their livings creating and selling traditional arts and clothing. For example, they sell about fifty thousand snowshoes every year.

In the next ten years, the Wyandotte Nation of Oklahoma also hopes to expand its fitness complex to include a swimming pool and an auditorium where movies, church events, and annual tribal meetings can be held. As part of their ten-year plan, they have also broken ground for building a retirement village and nursing home to better serve the elderly community.

After hundreds of years of hardship, it is in some ways amazing to see the hope and enthusiasm with which the different Wendat communities are now facing the future. In the last thirty years alone, ancestors of the Wendat people across North America have made remarkable progress in restoring their governments, reclaiming land, reestablishing community ties, preserving cultural heritage, increasing economic development, and advancing educational opportunities. Perhaps for the first time since Europeans invaded North America hundreds of years ago, it now seems that the Huron-Wendat and Wyandotte people have a bright future.

Further Reading

Bial, Raymond. *Lifeways: The Huron*. Tarrytown, N.Y.: Benchmark Books, 2001.

Bonvillain, Nancy. *The Huron*. New York: Chelsea House, 1989.

Gros-Louis, Max. *First among the Hurons*. Montreal, Québec: Harvest House, 1994.

Ridington, Jillian. *People of the Longhouse: How the Iroquoian Tribes Lived*. Buffalo, N.Y.: Firefly Books, 1995.

Schwabacher, Martin. *The Junior Library of American Indians: The Huron Indians*. New York: Chelsea Juniors, 1995.

Sioui, Georges E. *Huron/Wendat: The Heritage of the Circle*. East Lansing: Michigan State University Press, 1999.

Trigger, Bruce G. *The Huron Farmers of the North, Second Edition*. Belmont, Calif.: Wadsworth Group/Thomson Learning, 1990.

For More Information

Wendake Businesses
www.wendake.com

Wyandotte Communities
www.wyandotte.org/oklahoma

The Wyandot Nation of Kansas
www.ukans.edu/kansas/wn

The Wyandotte Nation of Oklahoma
www.wyandotte-nation.org

Sainte-Marie Among the Hurons
www.saintemarieamongthehurons.on.ca

Publisher's Note:

The Web sites listed on this page were active at the time of publication. The publisher is not responsible for Web sites that have changed their address or discontinued operation since the date of publication. The publisher will review and update the Web sites upon each reprint.

Glossary

aboriginal: Original or native to an area or country.

activists: People who work for a specific cause.

agriculturalists: People who make their living by farming the land.

allotments: Pieces of land divided up by the federal government and given to individuals or families.

assimilation: Absorption into another culture.

civil: Having to do with social structures and duties.

Colosseum: A huge, round, outdoor theater located in Rome, Italy.

communal: Held in common.

confederacy: A union of governments.

consensus: Agreement.

correspondence programs: Educational courses taught over distances using means such as the mail to transmit materials.

criteria: Standards on which decisions or judgments are made.

democratic: A form of government in which all people are supposed to have a voice or representation.

derogatory: Belittling and insulting.

diplomatically: With skill in listening and respectful negotiation.

displaced: Pushed out of one's original place.

distinguished: Set apart by excellence.

diverse: Having different characteristics.

economies: The systems of wealth.

ecosystems: Systems of natural environments.

elders: Wise and well respected senior members of the community.

facilitated: Got started or made easier.

federal civil service: The federal branch of public service.

First Nations: A term often used in Canada to refer to the Native people of North America.

fundamental: Most basic.

habitat: An area that supports life.

hieroglyphs: Ancient writings.

holocaust: Great or total destruction.

immunity: Natural resistance to disease.

inanimate: Not alive.

infamous: Having a bad reputation.

monarchy: A form of government with a king or queen as absolute ruler.

oil speculators: People who bought and sold oil and land containing oil for profit.

Parthenon: A temple to the Greek goddess, Athena, built between 447 and 432 B.C.

prejudices: Negative and unfair judgments made without knowing the facts.

reaffirming: Asserting again.

renaissance: A rebirth, especially of culture and artistic forms.

revolutionary: Something radically different from all things previously known.

riotous: Boisterous; loud and energetic to the point of being destructive.

scrolls: Rolls of parchment or papyrus containing writings.

sovereign: Independent and self-governing.

traditional: Based on beliefs, behaviors, or practices passed down through the generations in a specific culture or group.

unanimous: Supported by every person, all in agreement.

Western Hemisphere: The half of the earth comprised of North America, Mexico, Central America, and South America.

Index

Biographies

Autumn Libal is a graduate of Smith College. She is a freelance author and illustrator who lives in northeast Pennsylvania. She also authored *Folk Proverbs and Riddles,* in the Mason Crest series North American Folklore, as well as several titles for "Psychiatric Disorders: Drugs and Psychology for the Mind and Body."

Benjamin Stewart, a graduate of Alfred University, works as a freelance graphic artist and photographer. He traveled across North America to take the photographs included in this series.

Martha McCollough received her bachelor's and master's degrees in anthropology at the University of Alaska-Fairbanks, and she now teaches at the University of Nebraska. Her areas of study are contemporary Native American issues, ethnohistory, and the political and economic issues that surround encounters between North American Indians and Euroamericans.